OUR SOLAR SYSTEM

VENUS

Susan Ring

MEDIA ENHANCED BOOKS
AV2 BY WEIGL™
ADDED VALUE • AUDIO VISUAL

www.av2books.com

Go to **www.av2books.com**, and enter this book's unique code.

BOOK CODE

N 4 7 3 0 6 6

AV² by Weigl brings you media enhanced books that support active learning.

AV² provides enriched content that supplements and complements this book. Weigl's AV² books strive to create inspired learning and engage young minds in a total learning experience.

Your AV² Media Enhanced books come alive with...

Audio
Listen to sections of the book read aloud.

Key Words
Study vocabulary, and complete a matching word activity.

Video
Watch informative video clips.

Quizzes
Test your knowledge.

Embedded Weblinks
Gain additional information for research.

Slide Show
View images and captions, and prepare a presentation.

Try This!
Complete activities and hands-on experiments.

... and much, much more!

Published by AV² by Weigl
350 5th Avenue, 59th Floor
New York, NY   10118
Website: www.av2books.com   www.weigl.com

Library of Congress Cataloging-in-Publication Data
Ring, Susan.
Venus / Susan Ring.
    p. cm. -- (Our solar system)
Audience: 4-6.
Includes index.
ISBN 978-1-62127-270-0 (hardcover : alk. paper) -- ISBN 978-1-62127-279-3 (softcover : alk. paper)
1. Venus (Planet)--Juvenile literature. I. Title. II. Series: Our solar system (AV2 by Weigl)
QB621.R56 2014
523.42--dc23
                              2012044669

Printed in the United States of America in Brainerd, Minnesota
2 3 4 5 6 7 8 9 0 19 18 17 16 15

102015
131015

Project Coordinator Aaron Carr
Editorial BLPS Content Connections
Designer Mandy Christiansen

Every reasonable effort has been made to trace ownership and to obtain permission to reprint copyright material. The publishers would be pleased to have any errors or omissions brought to their attention so that they may be corrected in subsequent printings.

Photo Credits
Weigl acknowledges Getty Images as as its primary photo supplier for this title. Other sources: NASA: page 11 (Venus), NASA: page 16 (Venera 7).

Contents

Introducing Venus

There are three types of planets in the **solar system**: rocky planets, **Gas Giants**, and **Ice Giants**. Like Earth, Venus is a rocky planet, but the two planets are very different. The surface of Venus is almost entirely covered in volcanic rock from the planet's many active volcanoes. Venus rotates slowly. A day on Venus is about 243 days on Earth. Read on to discover more about this fascinating planet.

Venus is a hot planet. Its temperatures are high enough to melt some kinds of metal.

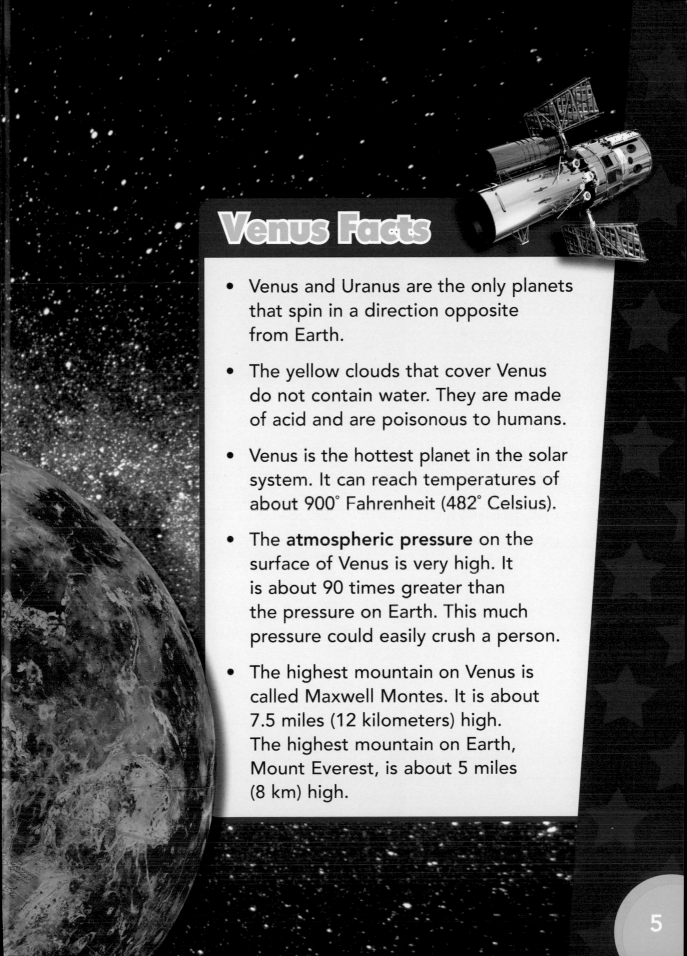

Venus Facts

- Venus and Uranus are the only planets that spin in a direction opposite from Earth.

- The yellow clouds that cover Venus do not contain water. They are made of acid and are poisonous to humans.

- Venus is the hottest planet in the solar system. It can reach temperatures of about 900° Fahrenheit (482° Celsius).

- The **atmospheric pressure** on the surface of Venus is very high. It is about 90 times greater than the pressure on Earth. This much pressure could easily crush a person.

- The highest mountain on Venus is called Maxwell Montes. It is about 7.5 miles (12 kilometers) high. The highest mountain on Earth, Mount Everest, is about 5 miles (8 km) high.

Naming the Planet

Venus is named after a Roman goddess. In Roman **mythology**, Venus is the goddess of love and beauty. In ancient times, the Romans built temples for this goddess. The Romans also honored Venus with festivals. These were known as the Vinalia festivals.

The planet was named after Venus because it shines so brightly in the night sky. The Romans compared the planet's bright light to the beauty of the goddess. The planet's glow can even be seen during the day.

In Roman mythology, Venus is the mother of Cupid.

Missing Moon

Venus and Mercury are the only two planets in the solar system that have no known moons. Some **astronomers** believe that Mercury was once Venus's moon. They think that Mercury broke away from Venus's **orbit**. This would explain why neither planet has a moon of its own.

Venus was also once thought to have a different moon. It was named Neith. A number of astronomers thought they saw Neith. Today, it is believed that the astronomers actually saw stars, not a moon.

Some scientists think Mercury and Venus do not have moons because of how close they are to the Sun. The pull of the Sun on these planets might mean that Mercury and Venus cannot hold a moon.

The Sun

Venus

First Sightings

Historical records show that people have observed Venus shining in the sky for thousands of years. Ancient people watched the movement of Venus and noticed its position in the sky. They could predict when it would rise and set. They knew when it would be close to Earth or far away.

The **Mayans** made a calendar based on the movement of Venus. The Mayan calendar was created thousands of years ago. Mayan astronomers observed Venus for many years before creating the calendar.

Scientists have discovered that the calendar the Mayans created was accurate in many ways. For example, it had a year of 365 days.

Twins in Space

The Mayans believed that Venus and the Sun were twin brothers. This was because Venus and the Sun rise and set at about the same time. They thought that Venus and the Sun protected the world from evil gods. It was believed that the two brothers were away fighting evil at night.

The Sun

The Mayans worshiped the Sun and Venus.

Venus

Spotting Venus

In ancient times, people called Venus the "morning star" and the "evening star." They thought the planet was two different stars. When Venus's orbit brings it toward Earth, the planet is known as the evening star. This is because it can be spotted in the evening sky. When the planet moves away from Earth, it is called the morning star. This is because it is the last star to be seen before sunrise.

Ancient astronomers named the morning star Phosphorus and the evening star Hesperus.

See for Yourself

You do not need a telescope to see Venus. It is one of the brightest objects in the sky. Only the Sun and Moon shine brighter. There is a reason why Venus is so bright. It is surrounded by thick clouds that reflect the Sun's light.

The clouds that make Venus look bright from Earth also make the planet's surface difficult to study.

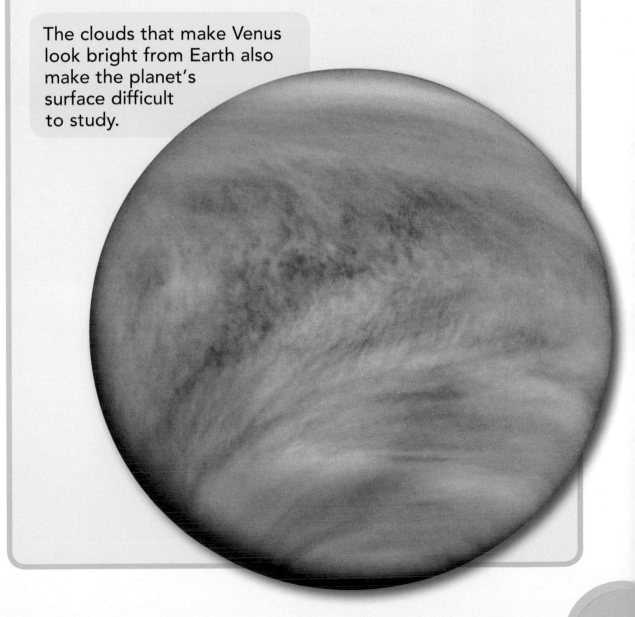

Charting Our Solar System

Earth's solar system is made up of eight planets, five known dwarf planets, and many other space objects, such as **asteroids** and **comets**. Venus is the second planet from the Sun.

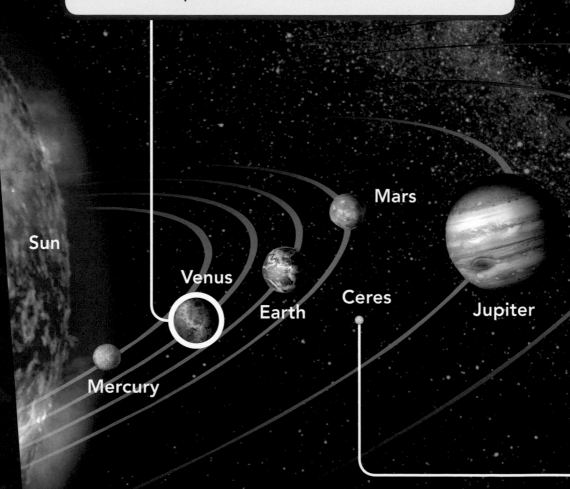

Sun

Mercury

Venus

Earth

Mars

Ceres

Jupiter

Order of Planets

Here is an easy way to remember the order of the planets from the Sun. Take the first letter of each planet, from Mercury to Neptune, and make it into a sentence. My Very Enthusiastic Mother Just Served Us Noodles.

Eris

Makemake

Haumea

Uranus

Pluto

Neptune

Saturn

Dwarf Planets

A dwarf planet is a round object that orbits the Sun. It is larger than an asteroid or comet but smaller than a planet.

Moons are not dwarf planets because they do not orbit the Sun directly. They orbit other planets.

Venus and Earth

People once thought that Venus had much in common with Earth. It was often called Earth's "twin sister." The planets are close in size and have almost the same amount of **gravity**. Scientists now know that the planets also have many differences. For example, the atmosphere on Venus is mostly carbon dioxide. On Earth, it is mostly nitrogen.

The Sun rises in the west on Venus and sets in the east. This is because Venus rotates in the opposite direction to Earth.

Venus's diameter
7,521 miles
(12,104 km)

Earth's diameter
7,926 miles
(12,756 km)

Comparing the Planets

Planets (by distance from the Sun)	Distance from the Sun	Days to orbit the Sun	Diameter	Length of Day	Mean Temperature
Mercury	36 million miles (58 million km)	88 Earth Days	3,032 miles (4,880 km)	1,408 hours	354°F (179°C)
Venus	67 million miles (108 million km)	225 Earth Days	7,521 miles (12,104 km)	5,832 hours	847°F (453°C)
Earth	93 million miles (150 million km)	365 Earth Days	7,926 miles (12,756 km)	24 hours	46°F (8°C)
Mars	142 million miles (228 million km)	687 Earth Days	4,217 miles (6,787 km)	24.6 hours	−82°F (−63°C)
Jupiter	484 million miles (778 million km)	4,333 Earth Days	88,732 miles (142,800 km)	10 hours	−244°F (−153°C)
Saturn	887 million miles (1,427 million km)	10,756 Earth Days	74,975 miles (120,660 km)	11 hours	−301°F (−185°C)
Uranus	1,784 million miles (2,871 million km)	30,687 Earth Days	31,763 miles (51,118 km)	17 hours	−353°F (−214°C)
Neptune	2,795 million miles (4,498 million km)	60,190 Earth Days	30,775 miles (49,528 km)	16 hours	−373°F (−225°C)

Venus Today

Astronomers have sent **space probes** into orbit around Venus to take pictures of the planet. It is difficult to study the planet's surface because of its thick clouds. Getting close to Venus has also been difficult. Venus's great atmospheric pressure has crushed several space probes.

Probes with **radar** equipment have gathered information without landing on Venus. One probe equipped with radar was the *Magellan*. From 1990 until 1994, it mapped much of Venus. More recently, the European Space Agency launched *Venus Express*. Its mission is to study the atmosphere of Venus from orbit.

Magellan
Launch 1989
Vehicle Orbiter

Venera 7
Launch 1970
Vehicle Lander

Mariner 2
Launch 1962
Vehicle Flyby

Messenger
Launch 2011
Vehicle Flyby

Venus Express
Launch 2005
Vehicle Orbiter

Akatsuki
Launch 2010
Vehicle Orbiter

Planet Watchers

Galileo Galilei discovered Venus's phases

The first astronomer to view Venus through a telescope was Galileo Galilei. In the 1600s, he made an important discovery about Venus. He noticed that the planet went through different **phases**, just like Earth's Moon. This is because the Sun shines on certain parts of the planet at different times. From Earth, only the parts of Venus that are lit by the Sun can be seen.

Italian astronomer Galileo Galilei began studying space through a telescope in 1610.

Carl Sagan researched high temperatures on Venus

Carl Sagan was born in New York City in 1934. He became interested in astronomy when he learned that the stars in the night sky were distant suns. He was an important astronomer in the second half of the 20th century.

In the early 1960s, people did not know what the surface of Venus was like. Some people even thought it could support life. Sagan's research showed that the high temperature on Venus was a result of the **greenhouse effect**. The *Mariner 2* mission confirmed this research. Nothing could live on or near the surface of Venus.

Carl Sagan helped design and manage some of the first missions to Venus in the 1960s.

What Have You Learned?

Take this quiz to test your knowledge of Venus.

1 Venus is the coldest planet. True or False?

2 What is the highest peak on Venus?

3 Who is Venus named after?

4 Why have some space probes been crushed upon approaching Venus?

5 Venus can be seen in the sky only during the evening. True or False?

6 Earth and Venus have a similar atmosphere. True or False?

7 How many moons does Venus have?

8 In what way is Venus similar to the moon?

9 Which planet is closer to the Sun: Venus or Mercury?

10 Which ancient people used Venus to help them create a calendar?

Answers

1. False. Venus is the hottest planet. 2. The highest peak on Venus is Maxwell Montes. 3. Venus is named after the Roman goddess of love and beauty. 4. Space probes have been crushed due to the high atmospheric pressure on Venus. 5. False. Venus can be seen in both the morning and evening. 6. False. Venus's atmosphere is mostly carbon dioxide. Earth's is mostly nitrogen. 7. Venus has no known moons. 8. Earth's moon and Venus both appear to go through different phases and shapes. 9. Mercury is closer to the Sun than Venus is. 10. The Mayans used Venus to create their calendar.

Young Scientists at Work

Greenhouse Effect Experiment

Venus's thick cloud layer traps heat. This is called the greenhouse effect. It makes the planet very hot. The Sun is closer to Mercury than Venus. Still, the greenhouse effect makes Venus hotter than Mercury. Try this experiment to find out why.

You will need:

- 2 thermometers
- 1 jar
- a lid for the jar or plastic wrap

1. Put one thermometer in the jar. Next, cover the jar with the lid or plastic wrap. Place the jar in a sunny area, next to the other thermometer.

2. After 30 minutes, look at the temperature showing on both thermometers. You will see that it is hotter inside the jar. This is similar to the greenhouse effect on Venus. Heat continues to enter, but none is let out.

Key Words

asteroids: small, solid objects in space that circle the Sun

astronomers: people who study space and its objects

atmospheric pressure: weight of the gases surrounding a planet

comets: small objects in space made from dust and ice

Gas Giants: large planets in the solar system made mostly of gas.

gravity: a force that pulls objects toward the center

greenhouse effect: a blanket-like effect in which gases trap heat, but do not let it out

Ice Giants: very cold giant planets.

Mayans: Native Americans who lived in southern Mexico and Central America

mythology: stories or legends, often about gods or heroes

orbit: the nearly circular path a space object makes around another object in space

phases: the appearance or shape of the Moon or a planet as seen from Earth

radar: equipment that uses radio waves to measure the distance and shape of objects

solar system: the Sun, the planets, and other objects that move around the Sun

space probes: spacecrafts used to gather information about space

Index

Log on to www.av2books.com

AV[2] by Weigl brings you media enhanced books that support active learning. Go to www.av2books.com, and enter the special code found on page 2 of this book. You will gain access to enriched and enhanced content that supplements and complements this book. Content includes video, audio, weblinks, quizzes, a slide show, and activities.

AV[2] Online Navigation

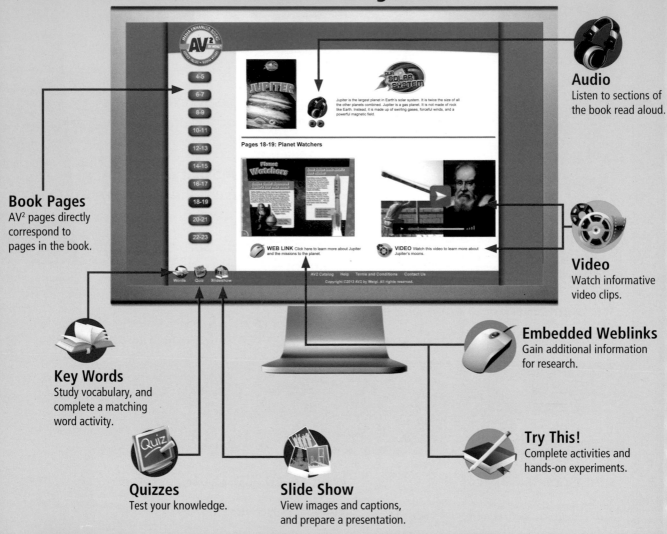

Book Pages
AV[2] pages directly correspond to pages in the book.

Audio
Listen to sections of the book read aloud.

Video
Watch informative video clips.

Key Words
Study vocabulary, and complete a matching word activity.

Embedded Weblinks
Gain additional information for research.

Try This!
Complete activities and hands-on experiments.

Quizzes
Test your knowledge.

Slide Show
View images and captions, and prepare a presentation.

AV[2] was built to bridge the gap between print and digital. We encourage you to tell us what you like and what you want to see in the future.

Sign up to be an AV[2] Ambassador at www.av2books.com/ambassador.